# WINTER

## AS THE EARTH TURNS

Lynn M. Stone

The Rourke Book Co., Inc.
Vero Beach, Florida 32964

Edited by Sandra A. Robinson


PHOTO CREDITS
All photos © Lynn M. Stone

**Library of Congress Cataloging-in-Publication Data**

Stone, Lynn M.
   Winter / by Lynn M. Stone.
      p.  cm. — (As the earth turns)
   Includes index.
   ISBN 1-55916-021-7
    1. Winter—Juvenile literature. [1. Winter.] I. Title.
II. Series: Stone, Lynn M.  As the earth turns.
QB637.8.S76  1994
508—dc20                             93-39059
                                           CIP

**Printed in the USA**                         AC

# TABLE OF CONTENTS

# WINTER

Winter is the coldest season. The calendar says winter begins on December 21. That is the day with the least daylight — the "shortest day of the year." In many parts of North America, winter weather begins much earlier than December 21.

Cold winter weather is hard on many animals and people. However, winter can also be a frigid, frozen world of beauty and a great time for sports.

*Slipping and sliding on a snowy hill is a joy of winter*

## THE SUN AND THE SEASONS

The sun is a fiery star. It supplies the Earth with heat and light as the Earth travels in its **orbit** around the sun.

The tilt of the Earth's poles causes the Earth's angle toward the sun to keep changing during its year-long orbit. This slowly changes the amount of sunlight that reaches Earth. As the amount of sunlight changes, the Earth's weather and seasons change, too.

After December 21, the periods of daylight begin to be longer.

*Changes in the Earth's angle toward the sun bring changes in the seasons*

# WINTER NORTH AND SOUTH

While you are on snow skis, people living in other parts of the world may be on water skis. Winter doesn't touch the entire Earth at once.

During our fall and winter, the Earth's northern **hemisphere,** or half, is tilted away from the sun. At the same time, the southern hemisphere is tilted toward the sun, and people there enjoy spring and summer. Later, the tilt is the opposite way.

*Winter grips the northern part of the world as the north pole tilts away from the sun*

## WINTER ARRIVES

Winter arrives with shortening days and frostings of snow. The wind tugs at leaves and sweeps branches bare. Skies become gray and dark.

By December the air has the cold bite of a steel trap. Snow lies in a soft, deep blanket over frozen ground. Rivers and lakes vanish under a lid of ice. Waterfalls freeze into giant icicles.

*Winter cold freezes waterfalls into glistening white beards*

*A squirrel rustles through snow to find a snack*

*For the heavily-furred Siberian tiger, winter is totally cool*

## BARE BRANCHES

Winter's short, cold days force plants to rest until early spring. The wide-leaved trees — like maples, oaks, beeches and elms — stand with naked winter branches.

The needle-leaved trees — the pines and spruces and their cousins — stay green under frost and snow. These trees are called **evergreens.**

Spring coaxes the wide-leaved trees back to life with longer, warmer days.

*A snowshoe rabbit, white in winter fur, crouches under the needle leaves of an evergreen*

# ANIMALS IN WINTER

Winter is the quiet season. Most birds have flown south, where winter is gentler and food is plentiful.

Animals that cannot fly away, hide. Frogs and toads bury themselves deep in mud. Woodchucks retreat to their burrows for a winter-long nap called **hibernation.** Squirrels and raccoons hide in cozy tree hollows.

Snowshoe rabbits and Arctic foxes hide safely with the help of their white fur coats.

*Covered with drops of dew, a bat in hibernation clings to a cave wall*

# TRACKS IN THE SNOW

Foxes, rabbits and some other animals stay active during the winter. Their tracks in the snow tell where they go — and why. The red fox's tracks follow a pheasant's. The wolf's trail follows a moose's.

The paw prints of a bounding **lynx** mix with a snowshoe rabbit's. The sharp hoof prints of deer fill a woodland where the deer chew bark from trees.

*Hunting for snowshoe rabbits, a lynx prowls in a northern forest*

# WINTER MEANS ...

Winter means a lonely red barn with snowdrifts all around. Winter means the glassy tinkle of an icy brook, the buzz of chickadees.

Winter means Christmas trees, snowmen, windows white with frost, and downy, falling snow. Winter means a puff of chimney smoke curling in the sky.

Winter means time to sled on a slippery hill or skate on a frozen pond. Winter means skiing in a white, wooded wonderland.

*Winter means the whisper of falling, blowing snow*

# WINTER AROUND THE WORLD

People who live fairly close to the **equator** don't have cold winters. The equator is not a huge heater. It is an imaginary line around the Earth's middle. That part of the world has little change in its angle toward the sun.

Even southern Florida is close enough to the equator to have weather that feels like summer almost all winter long.

## Glossary

**equator** (ee KWAY ter) — the imaginary line drawn on maps around the Earth's middle at an equal distance from the north and south poles

**evergreens** (EH ver greens) — trees that do not shed all of their leaves at once; they stay green all year

**hemisphere** (HEHM iss fear) — either the northern or southern half of the Earth, using the equator as a divider

**hibernation** (hi ber NAY shun) — a long, deep winter sleep during which an animal's normal body functions are slowed

**lynx** (LINKS) — a wildcat of the Northern woods, similar to the bobcat in size and appearance but with long ear tufts and heavily padded paws

**orbit** (OR bit) — the path that an object follows as it repeatedly travels around another object in space

# INDEX